D1634760

What people are saying about

Chill with Lil

I read this book with my 2 year old before bed every night as it's become an integral part of our bedtime routine. He's not really old enough to properly engage with the meditation, but he does the breathing and the soothing words and pictures really calm him down. He now asks for me to 'read Chill with Lil' and says 'bed time now' when we've finished. Absolute genius!
Miss Z. Rudder

What a beautiful gift for children! This book has all the ingredients to help your child relax before bedtime. It teaches your child to use imagination as a tool to help relax, feel at peace and listen to their body and mind (especially when they need to go to bed!). The illustrations and words are beautifully put together. Mindfulness and meditation need to be introduced to children of all ages, and this book is guaranteed to guide you onto that path.
Miss H J Dawe

This book is a great introduction to mindfulness techniques for children. It is a relaxing and thoughtful story that is perfect to calm little ones down after a busy day. The mindfulness techniques are introduced gently and subtly, and are easy to incorporate into a bedtime routine. I've found that it's helped my child to end the day in a relaxed and reflective way.
Rachel

My five year old struggles to wind down at bedtime….This book is a lovely story in itself about a child at bedtime with similarly recognisable problems! It then has the added helpful element of a practical calming exercise to really alter the mood. I like the way the mindfulness is not delivered by stealth...it is laid out as a separate exercise delivered by Aunt Lil. I think this is important...it gives the recipient reading child credit in being part of the decision to practice a calmer, meditative approach. My son now asks for this book to be read last as 'that one that should be read just before bed to calm me down'.
Lucy T.

Chill With Lil was nominated as one of Cygnus Book Club's star titles of 2018:

If you are a parent, grandparent or carer who struggles all the time with getting a child to sleep, this large format and full-colour picture book will be an invaluable tool to be read to the wide-awake child. It uses mindfulness techniques to induce calm and hopefully to encourage sleep. The pictures are bright, clear and charming – all the characters are cats and Lil is the aunt who comes in to save the day. There is also a page at the start specifically for the person reading the book that gives tips on what the book is trying to do and outlines the whole process of mindfulness.

4 3 0021717 1

Chill with Lil

A simple way to calm kids before bedtime using mindfulness techniques

Sue Pickford

*To those who helped
bring this book into the world.
Peace to all.*

First published in 2018 by Ragged Bears Ltd
Sherborne, DT9 3PH
www.ragged-bears.co.uk

ISBN: 978 185714 4710

Text & illustrations copyright © Sue Pickford 2018
Moral rights asserted

All rights reserved. No part of this publication may be reproduced, stored in or introduced
into a retrieval system, or transmitted in any form, or by any means, (electronic, mechanical,
photocopying, recording or otherwise) without prior written permission of the publisher.
Any person who does any unauthorized act in relation to this publication may be
liable to criminal prosecution and civil claims for damages.

A CIP catalogue record for this book
is available from the British Library

Printed and bound in China
on sustainably sourced paper

What is mindfulness?

In today's world, it's very easy to get caught up in a whirlwind of things to do and places to be. Stress can filter down to our children. Mindfulness can be a tool to help to calm children if they're upset, angry or confused. It can also enhance their attention and focus, and give them skills to develop their awareness and help them make better decisions. Mindfulness is attention to the present moment. It provides a chance to go to a safe, quiet place, and to come back a calmer, happier, more peaceful child.

About this book

This book introduces mindfulness ('chilling') with Lil. Lil helps to take Jake on a journey of relaxation and body-awareness using breathing techniques and visualisation. With a simple exercise for you to follow, this book has been developed to focus on the hour or so before bedtime, when energy needs to be slowed down ready for sleep. Many children get agitated around this time because they feel they're not ready, or are too tired to co-operate. By adding a pre-bedtime step of 'Chill with Lil' to your routine, you can noticeably change the pace. When the mind slows, the body naturally follows, and your child should enjoy the experience of quiet and stillness with your guidance (and so may you!). By keeping this softened energy constant until bedtime, you should find that your child is better prepared for a good night's sleep.

The whole story is only around ten minutes long, so it's quick and easy, and of course the beauty of mindfulness is that it can be used anytime and anywhere, not just before bedtime. So if your child ever needs calming before school, in the car, or even in the supermarket, then stop, be mindful, and suggest 'Let's chill with Lil'. Using the simple technique of breathing in and out slowly should settle them almost immediately. Be patient and reap the rewards!

About the author

Sue Pickford (aka Sue Cheung), is a children's author and illustrator who holds workshops and talks in schools around the UK. She is also a qualified meditation guide and an advocate for bringing mindfulness to children of all ages.

And now enjoy the book...

This is Jake.

Jake doesn't want to go to bed,
even though he feels tired.

He wants to stay up so he can...

build dens...

fight pirates...

drive tractors...

and jump off mountains.

"Come on Jake," says Mum.
"You've been playing all day. It's time for bed now."

But Jake does not want to put his pyjamas on
or brush his teeth.

no! he says.

And that's why Auntie Lil's coming round.
She has an idea.

Auntie Lil knows how to chill.

And she's going to show Jake.

"Jake, would you like to chill with Lil?" Mum asks.
Jake thinks this sounds fun.
Maybe it means he can stay up and play.

"Well, it's better than bedtime," says Jake.

*"First, let's put away your toys and make
sure everything is turned off,"* says Lil.

(Get ready to join in the exercise...)

"Now lie down on the floor and make yourself comfortable.

Put a blanket on to keep you nice and warm.

Are you ready?"
asks Lil.

"Ready to chill, Lil,"
says Jake.

Then in a slow and soft voice, Lil begins;
"Just copy me...

breathe in slowly
through the nose,

breathe out slowly
through the mouth,

breathe in slowly
through the nose,

breathe out slowly
through the mouth.

Now close your eyes.

What can you hear?"

Jake listens carefully.

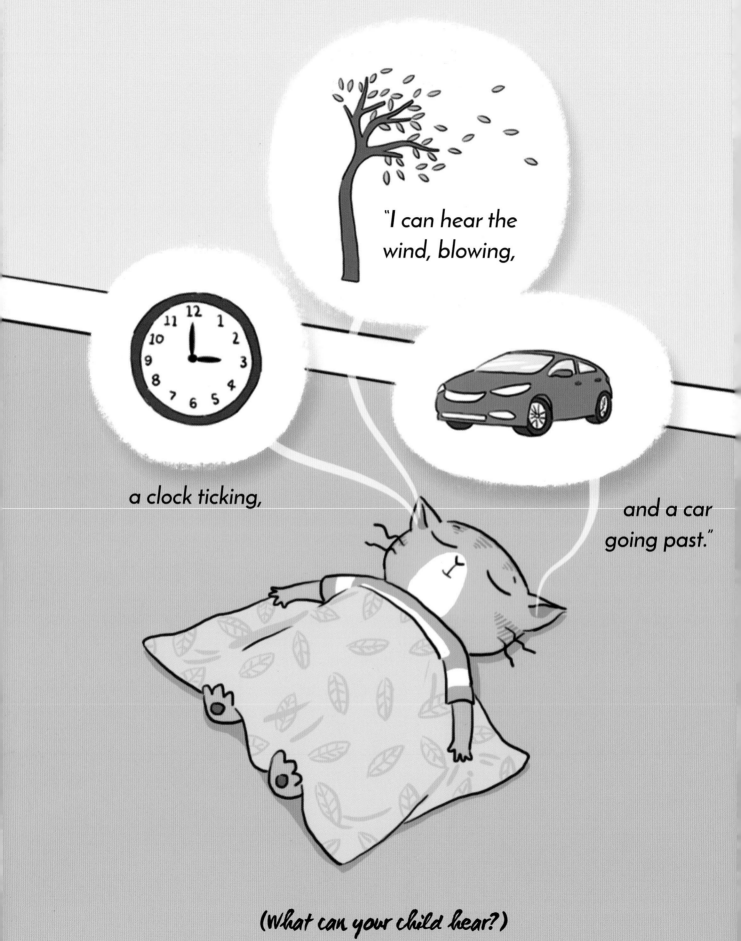

"I can hear the wind, blowing,

a clock ticking,

and a car going past."

(What can your child hear?)

"Good," whispers Lil.
"Now with your eyes still closed, I want you to
imagine you can hear the gentle waves of the sea.

You are lying on a beach on soft, warm, golden sand.

The sun shines brightly in the sky above.
You can feel the heat of the sun all over your body.

You are relaxed, calm and safe.

Feel the warmth of the sun on your toes, one by one.

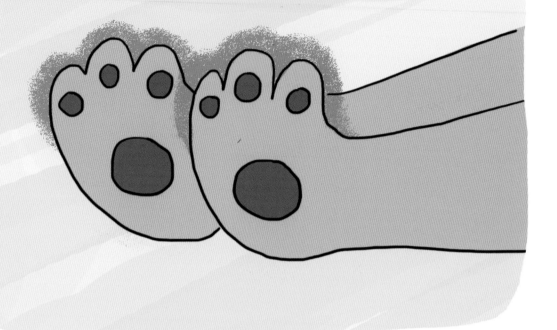

The warm feeling spreads to your feet.

Relax your feet and let your heels sink into the sand underneath.

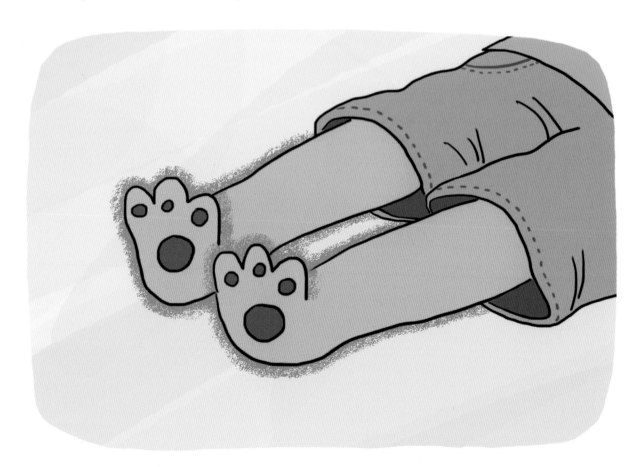

The warmth of the sun spreads into your tummy
and all around your back.
Feel your back sink into the soft, soft sand.

The heat warms your chest, neck and shoulders.

Feel your shoulders relax gently into the golden sand
underneath you.

Feel the warm glow wrap around your arms as it moves
down to your elbows, your wrists and your hands.

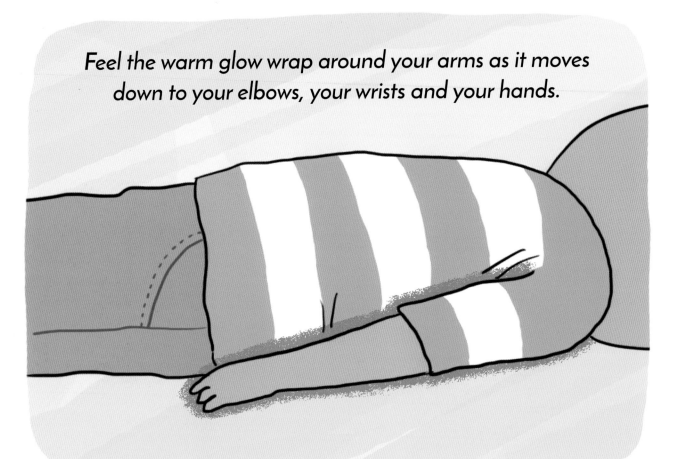

The heat flows slowly into
each of your fingers.

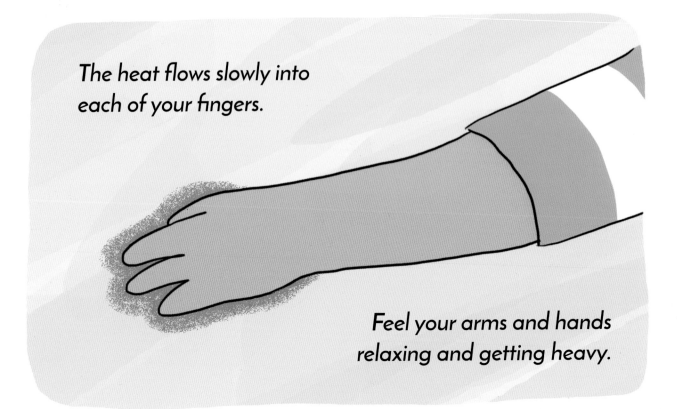

Feel your arms and hands
relaxing and getting heavy.

You can feel the warmth on your face now.
Soften your eyes.
Soften your mouth.

Now relax even more
and soften your
whole face.

Your head is now
heavy and relaxed.

Your whole body is now
heavy and relaxed.

You can still hear the gentle waves of the sea, and palm trees swaying quietly in the breeze.

You can hear songbirds flying overhead.

22

One of the songbirds glides down and lands next to you.
It sings softly into your ear:

"It's time to go now."

Then you listen to the beat of its wings,
as it flies off into the distance.

Now it's time for you to come back.

Gently wiggle your fingers and toes.
Gently move your arms and legs.
Turn your head slowly to the right,
now turn it slowly to the left.
Turn it to the right again,
to the left,
and back to the middle.

*breathe in slowly
through the nose,*

*breathe out slowly
through the mouth,*

*breathe in slowly
through the nose,*

*breathe out slowly
through the mouth.*

Now open your eyes.
(This is the end of the exercise)

How do you feel?" asks Lil.
"Nice and calm and peaceful," smiles Jake.

"Chilled?" says Lil.
"Chilled," says Jake.

Still chilled,
Jake puts on
his pyjamas,

and brushes his teeth.

Auntie Lil tucks him into bed and kisses him goodnight.

"Doesn't your bed feel lovely, soft and warm,
just like when you were lying on the beach?" says Lil.

"Yes," says Jake, sleepily.

28

Then Mum reads him a story.
And Jake goes straight to sleep.

Goodnight.

Other Ragged Bears books that you might enjoy!

Try and Say Abracadabra!
9781857144680 • £11.99

All Except Winston
9781857144734 • £11.99

Somewhere Out There, Right Now
9781857144765 • £7.99

My Magic
9781857144758 • £12.99